CELIUS DOUGHERTY

30 ART SONGS
in original keys

FOR MEDIUM/HIGH VOICE AND PIANO

ISBN 0-634-06970-5

G. SCHIRMER, Inc.

DISTRIBUTED BY

HAL•LEONARD®
CORPORATION

7777 W. BLUEMOUND RD. P.O. BOX 13819 MILWAUKEE, WI 53213

CELIUS DOUGHERTY

1902 — 1986

"I love poetry. I love what poetry suggests to me in the way of music.
The first thing that I wrote was a song. When I was seven years old I wrote a song."

American composer, accompanist, and duo-pianist Celius Dougherty was born in Glenwood, Minnesota, into a family so musical that his music teacher/church choirmaster mother organized her seven children into a band. His first public performance, at age ten, was as accompanist for one of his mother's song recitals. After graduating from the University of Minnesota, he moved to New York to study piano and composition at Juilliard. He soon became a sought-after recital accompanist, touring Europe and making RCA records with the great Russian baritone Alexander Kipnis, Canada's adventurous Eva Gauthier, and Sweden's Povla Frijsch, whom he admired for her interpretive abilities.

In 1939 Dougherty formed a two-piano team with Vincenz Ruzicka, appearing in every US state and in Vienna with the Vienna Symphony in 1955. The duo was noted for giving world premieres of important new works for two pianos: Hindemith's *Sonata for Two Pianos*, Stravinsky's *Sonata for Two Pianos*, Berg's *Suite from Lulu*, Schönberg's *Variations on a Recitative*. Some of these were works for orchestra, which he arranged for two pianos. Another was a sonata, which he arranged from nautical themes, *Music from Seas and Ships*, dedicated to his brother Ralph, who went down with the USS Arizona at Pearl Harbor.

Dougherty's catalogue of compositions includes a one-act opera for children, *Many Moons*, based on a story by James Thurber, as well as a piano concerto, a string quartet, and sonatas for violin, piano, and piano duo. But he is best remembered for 200 gracious and witty songs. His early songs were settings of English and American poets: Walt Whitman, e.e. cummings, Amy Lowell, Robert Frost, and Siegfried Sassoon. Later songs derived from essays by children, Chinese poetry, the dictionary, newspapers, spirituals and folksongs.

Further information on this publication, the availability of other works, performances, and background on the composer may be found at www.celiusdougherty.org.

Contents

Composing Art Song

by Celius Dougherty

The aspect of song writing that is so interesting to me is the influence which poetry exerts upon the music. Actually, I have never believed that music should *need* to be talked about, that it should make itself understood on its own terms. Matisse said this about art: "A work of art should contain within itself its own explanation." I believe this too. Yet it can be interesting, particularly to the interpreter of the song, to know what it was about the poem that impelled the composer to set it to music.

When I look over the texts of the songs I have written, I can see that there are certain very definite qualities in poetry that have attracted me and that have given me a kind of cue towards a musical setting. Of course, the most obviously adaptable poem to set to music is the one that makes a direct reference to music or to singing, poems in which one sees that the poet is already thinking of them in terms of song. I also find that I am attracted to poems in which some kind of dramatic experience is set forth. Sometimes this can take the form almost of a miniature libretto, which was the case for me with "Madonna of the Evening Flowers."

There is another kind of poem that appeals to me. Since the piano is the instrument I know best, I often like to make use of the accompaniment to play some unusual role. In "A Minor Bird" I attempted to imitate on the piano the song of the mourning dove. In "little fourpaws" I tried to suggest the soft footsteps of some little four-footed animal. And so on.

I am stimulated by poems that suggest some unusual musical form (unusual for a song), such as a fugue, or a theme and variations, or a sonatina, or a passacaglia (as in "little fourpaws").

There are always those poems which begin with some irresistible line that strikes one simply with the beauty of its language and compels one to attempt to match that in music. I also find that I am frequently attracted to a curious kind of poem in which the thought takes an unexpected turn, often times as late as the very last line. This can be a difficult challenge, for one has to say something new at the end of the song, and yet the listener must be prepared for it so that it will still be contained within the frame of the song. This was the case with the Robert Frost poem, "A Minor Bird," with its unexpected and philosophical conclusion, and also with Bret Harte's "What the Bullet Sang," with its disturbing last line that casts a shadow over all that has gone before.

Finally, I am attracted to and stimulated by poems in which our language is used in some unconventional way. "Sound the Flute!" by William Blake was one of these, with its lines of only three syllables. The poems of e.e. cummings feature unusual turns, in which the poet often reverses the order of the words, not so much from the desire to be novel as for the purpose of giving a fresh meaning and emphasis to familiar words, making one think about them in a new light.

These are some of the ways that poetry has appealed to me as a composer. No doubt other composers would have just as many and different reasons for setting poetry. It would be interesting to know.

This article and the following remarks were adapted from writings and recorded spoken comments by the composer, and from correspondence between Celius Dougherty and Judy Bender.

THE COMPOSER'S REMARKS ON SELECTED SONGS

e.e. cummings songs:
little fourpaws
o by the by
thy fingers make early flowers
until and i heard
poems by e.e. cummings

Although these songs set to poems of e.e. cummings are not in any sense to be considered a cycle, still, they are connected by virtue of their unique language. They also share a certain romantic attitude. It was in the original use of language that I felt stimulated into new channels of thinking. A habit of cummings' is to introduce seemingly unessential words into his lines, as in the second line here:

> until and i heard
> a certain a bird

He might have said, "until I heard a certain bird," but by adding these little words "and" and "a," he gives the lines a freer rhythm and a more musical cadence. Actually, this is not an innovation in poetry. Shakespeare did the same thing, such as in these verses from The Winter's Tale:

> When that I was
> And a little tiny boy
> With heigh ho
> The wind and the rain.

He could have said, "When I was a little tiny boy," but he introduced the words "that" and "and" just as cummings did, giving his lines freer play.

"until and i heard" is a charming comparison of the song of a bird to the poet's own singing, very much to the advantage of the bird. In "little fourpaws" a small child is grieving over the death of a little pet, wondering where and why it has gone. In "o by the by" a small boy is flying his kite, a symbol of childhood's dreams. Even though the kite seems to disappear into the blue sky, the child holds the end of the string and does not let go. In other words, he hangs onto the dreams that grown people let out of their grasp. "thy fingers make early flowers" is a beautiful, lyric poem very much in the manner of many early English lyrics such as "Go, Lovely Rose," or poems of Robert Herrick, or even Elizabeth Barrett Browning. [Dougherty also set two further cummings poems, not included in this volume: "O Thou to whom the musical white spring," and "i thank You God."]

Declaration of Independence
poem by Wolcott Gibbs

This song is not what the title leads you to expect. It is based on the words of a small boy, which I found in The New Yorker. The boy's father related, "My four-year-old son has made up a song, or a poem, or something, that he sings every night in his bathtub. It goes on practically forever, like the Old Testament, and I have been able to copy down only a part of it. But even this fragment seems to me to be one of the handsomest literary efforts of the year, as well as proof that children are the really pure artists with complete access to their thoughts, and no foolish reticence. I think seldom has the vision of any heart's desire been put down so explicitly." I wished to give the vocal line a certain resemblance to the monotony and repetitiveness of any small child's singing. And then I have let the piano comment on the child's rebellious ideas.

Everyone Sang
poem by Siegfried Sassoon

The very title of this poem would have appeal for setting to music. But there was more to it, for there was a different kind of singing implied here. The subtitle is "Armistice Day, 1918." Siegfried Sassoon had gone eagerly into World War I, but soon became disillusioned and wrote, while he was still in the trenches, his bitter poems denouncing war. In this poem he expresses his exultation at the end of the hostilities and the coming of peace. I felt that I wanted to express this too, for I remembered that Armistice Day and the special meaning it had for me. But it seemed to me that the poem was timeless; it need not be limited to 1918. It could express the joy of all at the cessation of war.

Green Meadows
poem by Celius Dougherty

I wrote this for Gertrude Hull, a voice professor at the University of Minnesota whom I accompanied. In 1923 she took a selection of my songs to New York and showed them to Mr. Sonneck, the director of publications there [at G. Schirmer], from which he chose "Green Meadows" for publication. He also wrote to Miss Hull a detailed description of the faults and merits of the other songs. That was very valuable and useful to me. G. Schirmer has remained my "main-stay" throughout my career – and I can never forget Miss Hull's role in making it so.

Hush'd be the camps today
poem by Walt Whitman

I value this song perhaps more than anything I have written. I feel I succeeded best in accomplishing what I wanted to do. I usually know poems for years before I set them. But this one struck me the minute I read it, and I was impelled to set it immediately. It seemed not only a eulogy of Lincoln, but of Franklin D. Roosevelt, and of my own brothers, who fell in France and in Pearl Harbor. I am a slow worker, but this time I seemed to have help from a higher source, and the song was ready in a few days.

The K'e
anonymous Chinese poem, 718 B.C.

The text comes from a collection of ancient Chinese poems, translated with great beauty by the English scholar Helen Waddell. I was attracted to this particular poem, not only because of the touching story it has to tell of a woman's first love and her betrayal, but because of the extraordinary method of understatement by which the story is told. Through the great craft of the Chinese poets this tragedy of a life is distilled into a few terse lines. The result seems almost artless. The language is of the utmost simplicity; each phrase of the story is stated without comment, as though the woman had ceased to have feelings.

Here was the challenge: to find music that would be expressive of the tragic theme, but would not overstep the emotional limits established by the poem. I did not attempt a precise imitation of Chinese music, preferring to let its character emerge, if possible, through the simple, folk-like theme that I chose and the most sparse harmonic background: four base notes, harmonized by empty fourths and fifths.

Love in the Dictionary

The precedent of writing amusing songs has been established long ago. Even the most serious composers have had the urge to write something in a light-hearted vein, and have even considered it a challenge. We know how Brahms admired Johann Strauss, and how Beethoven admired Rossini. Witty songs are always welcomed by the audience, but I think the audience cannot realize how difficult they are to write. One problem is to find an appropriate text that suggests music. Another, as in the case of this song, is to mold the rather loosely constructed words into a form that has musical validity. The listener may not be aware of the composer's procedure, but he or she will instinctively know whether or not it succeeds. The idea for this song was given to me by a friend who suggested that I attempt something different in the way of a love song. He proposed looking up the word "love" in the dictionary, which I did. I found there a series of definitions, which I have used exactly as they appeared, word for word.

Loveliest of trees
poem by A.E. Housman

You are surely familiar, as I am, with the many attractive settings of this beautiful poem by Housman. I had never thought to add another setting to these, but since we know there is no limit to the ways in which a poem can be set (there are many interesting examples of this in vocal literature), I felt there was an aspect of the text which had not been emphasized: the tremulous emotion one feels at the sight of the cherry trees in bloom, a feeling of suspension in space. When I played this song for my publisher, the editor said, "There you go again writing songs nobody can sing." However, it has been sung by more singers than any one of my songs, and by every kind of voice (Bidu Sayao, Blanche Thebom, William Warfield, Leontyne Price, etc.).

Madonna of the Evening Flowers
poem by Amy Lowell

This is a poem that interested me because of its dramatic content. Actually, it has the character almost of a miniature libretto for a little opera, sung by a single character. The poet is represented here as tired from the day's work, coming home, calling for his beloved. There is no answer; the house is quiet and apparently deserted. The poet calls again, becoming a little more concerned, even apprehensive, and begins to go about searching. Suddenly the beloved is seen, standing in the garden with a basket of flowers on her arm, and surrounded by Canterbury bells that seem to the poet to be playing little tunes. Unaware of the anxiety that she has caused, she starts to speak quite prosaically of things that need to be done about the garden. But the poet is transfixed, and sees the beloved as in a vision, as a kind of Madonna. His only thought is to kneel before her in adoration. Now all about them the Canterbury bells, instead of playing little tunes, are thundering forth in loud "Te Deums." This reference to the section of the Mass suggested to me a theme that could become an integral part of the song, the Gregorian setting of the words "Te Deum," which has been used so wonderfully by so many composers. This gave a kind of devotional character to the song, and I found myself thinking of it as an evening vespers, with the Madonna, the flowers, the bells, and the music all combining to compel the poet's adoration. At the same time, it is a dramatic scene, beginning with quite free recitative, developing slowly, and gradually taking the form of an aria.

A Minor Bird
poem by Robert Frost

This poem attracted me by its title, and thus gave me the opportunity to use a birdcall. In this case it is a particular kind of birdcall, which by its repetitive nature became inviting to the poet, but which caused him finally to philosophize over the whole subject of song. Here is the poet being annoyed by a bird's repeated song. When he tried to frighten the bird away in order not to hear its song anymore, it occurs to him that it may not be the bird's fault that his song was pitched in this minor key. From this he arrives at the beautiful conclusion that every song, however unwelcome it may be to us, has its reason for being, and it is not for us to wish to silence it. I have no way of knowing which bird Robert Frost had in mind when he wrote this poem. For me, it suggested one that I have known from early childhood, the mourning dove, which seemed to me was always singing in the key of F minor. I let this minor theme dominate the whole first half of the song. Then, at the end, I turned it into a major key for a moment to show that it could be beautiful, too, and that it really would be wrong to silence it.

Portrait
poem by Robert Browning

The poem just asked for music. Browning's texts are so concentrated they seem to invite laboration.

Primavera
poem by Amy Lowell

This amusing poem was given to me by Eva Gauthier. Eva was greatly admired by Amy Lowell, who often entertained her when she sang in Boston, and made her presents of her books of poems. Here was a different kind of poem about spring. Mrs. Lowell has discovered that spring has arrived ahead of schedule. She pokes fun at those who determine everything by the calendar, and then she proceeds to offer her evidence that she has seen the spring before the 21st of March. I was attracted to the informality of the text (free verse), but wondered why she gave her poem the title "Primavera" instead of "Spring." I knew that Amy Lowell was greatly influenced by music in her writing. Her poetry is full of references to music; she even tried to approximate in words the dissonances of Stravinsky and Bartok. The fact that the title was in Italian led me to think of the poem in terms of Italian music, and naturally, opera. I found that the conversational character of the words fell easily into the recitative form, which, in turn, led into an aria. In other words, it is a kind of mock-operatic scene transplanted from Italy to Boston.

Serenader
poem by George Dillon

George Dillon is one of the Chicago group of poets that, along with Sherwood Anderson, Vachel Lindsay and Carl Sandburg, flourished in the early 1920s. I was attracted, of course, to a poem called "Serenader," as well as to its pure poetic quality. Yet this was not a serenade in the usual sense. The poet is singing, not to seek the favors of a loved one, but rather, to make us the humble offering of a song. This seemed to me a fresh approach to the word "serenade." He takes what we normally think of as a classical and even dated instrumental form, and gives it modern validity. This is the contemporary American poet justifying his vocation. For me, it is an ideal illustration of the need of the poet or musician to write.

Sound the Flute!
poem by William Blake

Here is a poem that suggested music by its very title. But its chief interest for me was the extraordinarily short lines, the shortest I have ever seen in a poem. None of them are longer than three syllables, a device admirably suited to the subject of this poem, which concerns itself with little things.

Weathers
poem by Thomas Hardy

Here is a poem of strong contrasts. There are just two stanzas, one depicting a spring day in the English countryside, in which the cuckoo, the nightingale, young girls and travelers are all lured out into the sun, and people begin to dream of going to the South or the West. The other stanza depicts the depressing effect of this countryside in dripping wetness and fog, which sends birds, shepherds and other people back into their homes. The contrast of mood was the thing that appealed to me here. In order to emphasize this still further, I allowed myself great liberty. I returned to the first half of the poem, repeating it entirely. Ordinarily, I do not approve of repeating a single line or even a word of a poem (if the poet has not already done so), and yet here I repeated half of the poem. But by doing this, I felt I was able to heighten the contrasts in the text, as well as end the song on a cheerful note. I hope you will feel that I was justified.

What the Bullet Sang
poem by Bret Harte

Here I saw the chance to suggest in the piano the "drive" of a bullet, through reiteration of a single note against harmonic changes that never "deflect" it from its course.

BEAUTY IS NOT CAUSED

Emily Dickinson

Celius Dougherty

Poem from *The Further Poems of Emily Dickinson*, reprinted by permission of Little Brown and Company

ceas-es, Chase it not and it a - bides, _____

O - - - - - ver-take the creas-es _____ in the

mead-ow _____ when the wind runs _____ its _____ long fin - gers

espressivo

DECLARATION OF INDEPENDENCE

Wolcott Gibbs

Celius Dougherty

cause he does not care to. And when they tell him___ to eat his

din-ner, he will just laugh at them,___ And he will

not take his nap, be-cause he does not wish to.___ He will

just sit there in the noon - day sun.

He will go a - way__ and play with the Pan - - da,

And when they come to look for him, He will

stick them with spears and put them in the gar - bage and put the

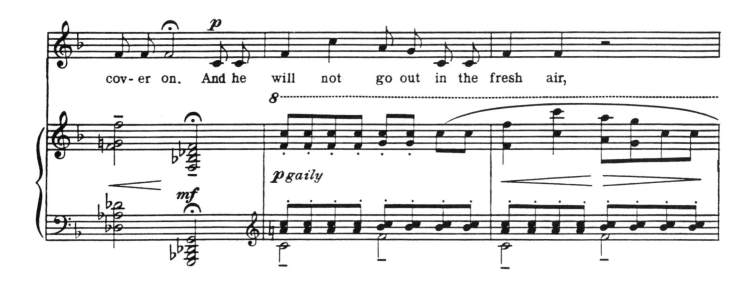

cov - er on. And he will not go out in the fresh air,

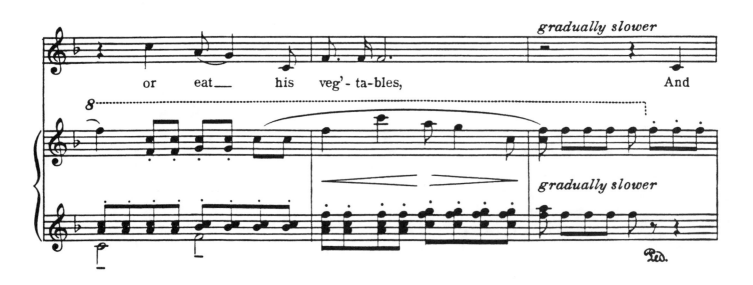

or eat___ his veg'- ta- bles, And

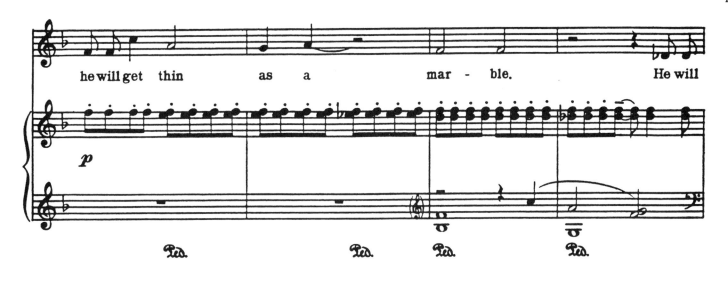

he will get thin as a mar - ble. He will

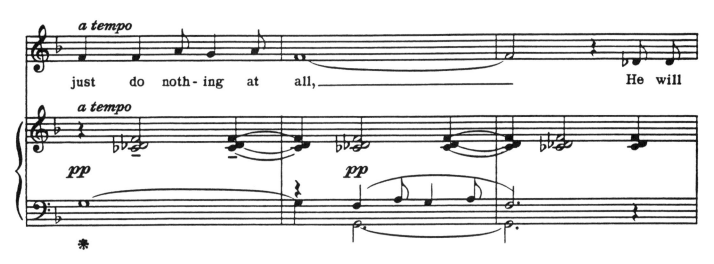

just do noth - ing at all,_____ He will

just sit there in the noon - day sun._____

THE BIRD AND THE BEAST

The Atlantic Monthly*

Celius Dougherty

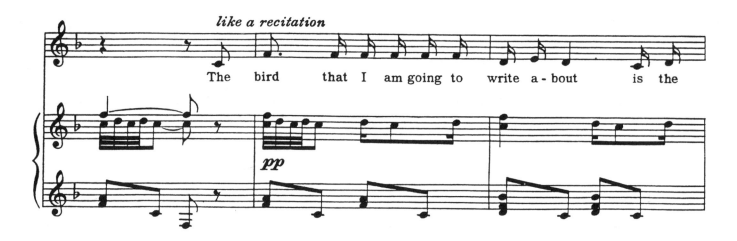

*Taken from Sir Ernest Gowers "Plain Words". Used by permission of The Atlantic Monthly.

all by day, and at night is as blind as a bat.

I do not know much a - bout the owl, so I will go on to the

beast that I am going to choose. It is the cow.

The cow is a mam-mal. It has six sides, right, left, an up-per and be-low, At the back it has a tail on which hangs a brush. With this it sends the flies a-way, so they

a tempo

p

don't fall in - to the milk. The head is for the pur-pose of

grow - ing horns, and so that the mouth can be some-where. The

horns are to butt with, and the mouth is to moo with.

Un - der the cow hangs the milk. It is ar-ranged for

milk - ing. When peo - ple milk, the milk comes, there is

nev - er an end to the sup - ply. How the cow does it I have

(rit.)

nev-er re - al - ized, but it makes more and more. And

what it eats it____ eats twice, so that it gets e -

nough.____ The cow has a fine sense of smell. You can

smell it far a - way.

This is the rea - son for the fresh air in the coun - try.

When it is hun - gry it

moos. And when it says noth - ing

pp

it is be - cause its in - side is

all full up with grass. *rit.* *Slowly*

p

THE CHILDREN'S LETTER TO THE UNITED NATIONS

Public School No. 90
Queens, New York

Celius Dougherty

With fervent conviction

War____ is fight-ing. Peo-ple hate and take peo-ple's clothes a-way. They should think not to make a war. They should-n't have guns.____ In

Sun-day-school they say: "Thou shalt not kill".___ In Sun-day-school they say: "Thou shalt not kill"._____ War is fight-ing. Peo-ple hate and take peo-ple's clothes a-way. They should think not to make a war. They should-n't have guns.

26

hors - es and lambs,___ and ap - ple trees and pear trees and peach trees

too,___ and train the peo-ple to make things, to be___ a bar - ber, to

learn to be a bar - ber and things like that?

With greater solemnity

Please ask God___ to kind - ly make us bet - ter,

EVERYONE SANG
(Armistice Day)

Siegfried Sassoon

Celius Dougherty

THE FIRST CHRISTMAS

Elizabeth Fleming   Celius Dougherty

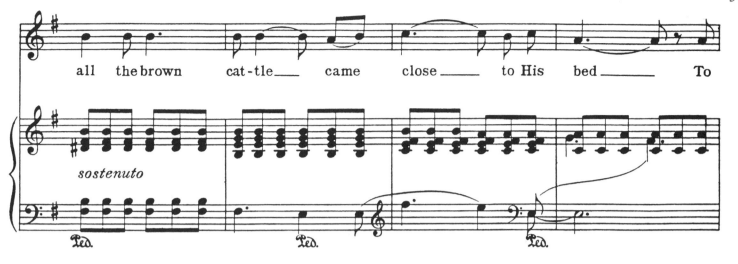

all the brown cat-tle___ came close___ to His bed___ To

sostenuto

see the wee___ Ba - by a - sleep in__ their shed,___ To

see the wee___ Ba - by a - sleep in their shed.___

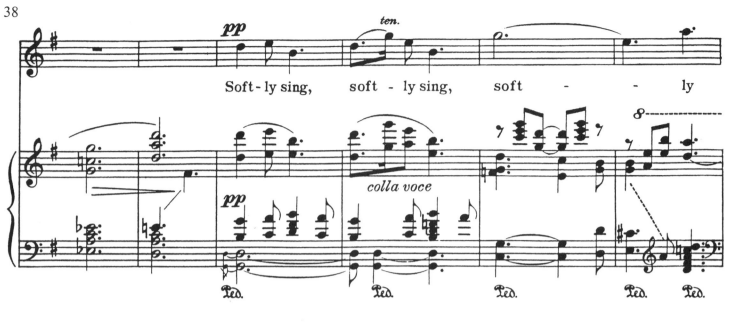

Soft-ly sing, soft-ly sing, soft - ly

sing._____ His car - ols were

prais - es of love and good will _____ That rose ___ in the

mid - night, so calm and _ so still, To her - ald the ear - li-est

Christ - mas we know, _____ When Je - sus was lit - tle, a

long while a - go, _____ When Je - sus was lit - tle, a

p

con pedale

long   while a - go._____

Soft - ly sing,   soft - ly sing,   soft - - ly

pp

ten.

colla voce

sing._____

pp   *pp*   *pp*

THE K'E *

From the Chinese
718 B. C.

Celius Dougherty

*Pronounced *kay*

wife; I had your word. And so I

took the road with you, And cross the

ford. I do not

GREEN MEADOWS

C.D.

Celius Dougherty

Thro' mead-ows green I wan-der'd, in the dusk, Be-side the si-lent stream;____ By shad-ed

paths, in wood-lands dark-en-ing, I long for one a-part, _____ for one a-part. O eve-ning fair with skies of blue a-bove, O

star - ry night, O moon of sil - ver light,_____ My

ach - ing heart doth yearn! Love - ly night, thou

art my own— Ah! must I love thee a - lone?

HUSH'D BE THE CAMPS TODAY

Walt Whitman

Celius Dougherty

And each— with mu-sing soul re-

tire— to ce-le-brate, our dear com - man - der's

death.——

No more for him _____ life's stormy con-flicts, Nor vic-to-ry, nor de-feat; no more time's dark e-vents, charg-ing like ceaseless clouds ___ a-cross the sky. _____ But sing, po-et, ___ in our

Sing _____

as they

close the doors of earth up - on him—

Sing _____ one verse,

little fourpaws

e.e. cummings

Celius Dougherty

LOVE IN THE DICTIONARY *

Celius Dougherty

* From Funk and Wagnalls Students' Standard Dictionary

per-son-al at-tach-ment, caus - ing one to ap-pre - ci-ate,

de - light__ in, or crave_____ the pres-ence

or pos-ses - sion__ of the ob - ject,

and to please _____ and pro - mote the wel - fare __ of that

ob - ject;   de - vot - ed   af - fec - tion   or at-

tach - ment;   spe - cif - ic - al - ly: the feel - ing

LOVELIEST OF TREES

A. E. Housman

Celius Dougherty

From "A Shropshire Lad" reproduced by permission of Henry Holt & C? Inc.

wood - land ride
Wear-ing white for East - - er-
- tide.

Now, of my three score-years and ten, Twen - ty will not

come a-gain, And take from se-ven-ty springs a score, It

MADONNA OF THE EVENING FLOWERS

Amy Lowell

Celius Dougherty

All day long I have been work-ing

Now I am tired. I call: "Where

are you?" But there is on-ly the oak tree rust-ling in the

Words reprinted by permission of the publishers, Houghton Mifflin Company.

wind.   The house is ve - - ry qui - - et.

più p   *pp*

mp

The sun shines in on your books, On your

p sustained, expressively

scis-sors and thim-ble just put down, But you are not there.

mf

mf

Sud-den-ly   I am lone - ly: Where

(more intensely)

mf

73

A MINOR BIRD

Robert Frost

Celius Dougherty

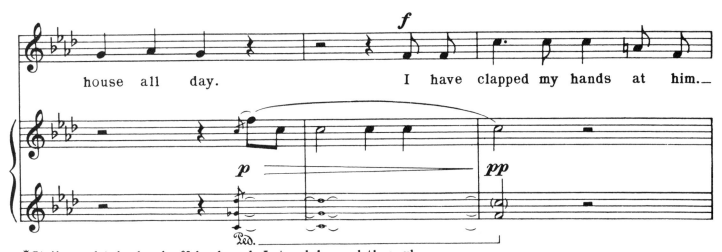

*Strike and take hand off keyboard. Let pedal sound through.

From COMPLETE POEMS OF ROBERT FROST. Copyright, 1930, 1949, by Henry Holt and Co., Inc., 1936, 1948, by Robert Frost. By permission of Henry Holt and Co., Inc., and Jonathan Cape, Ltd.

from the door   When it seemed as if I could bear no more.

The   fault must part-ly have

been   in   me,_____ The   bird was not to   blame for his

key._____

And be-sides there must be   some-thing

wrong _____   In   want-ing to si - lence an - y   song._____

o by the by

e.e. cummings

Celius Dougherty

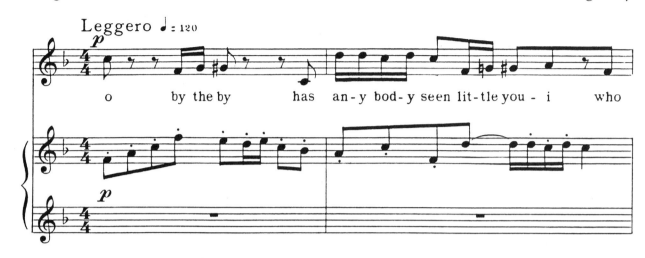

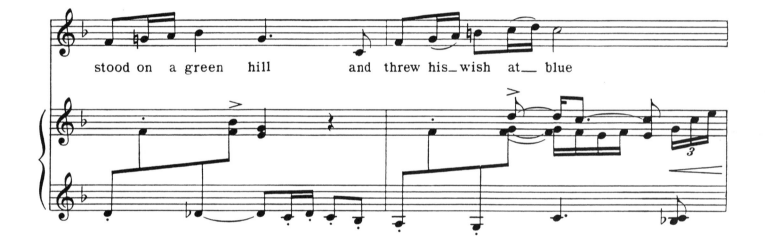

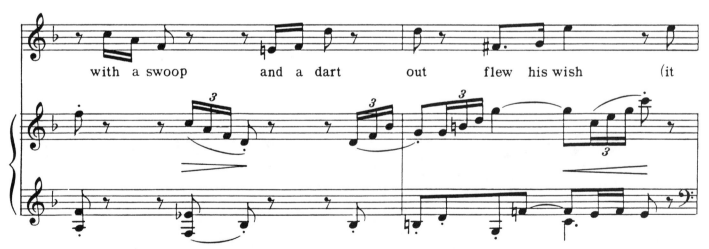

dived   like a fish   but it   climbed like a   dream)

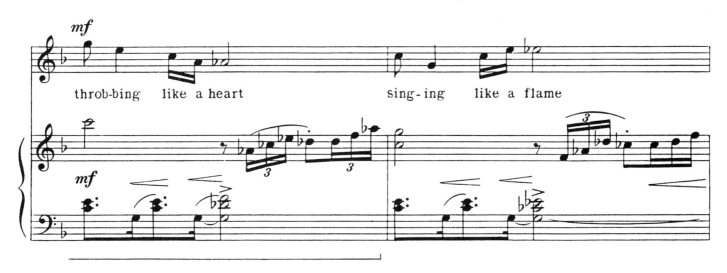

throb-bing   like a heart   sing-ing   like a flame

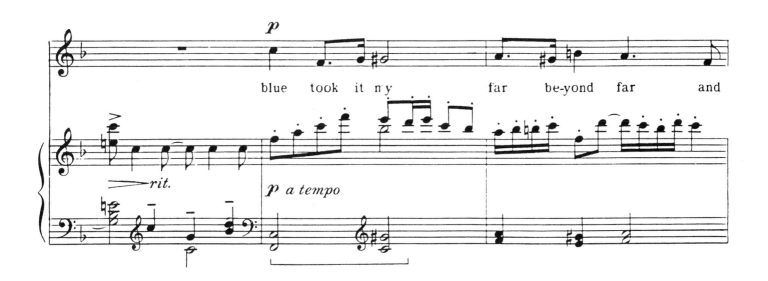

blue   took it my   far   be-yond far   and

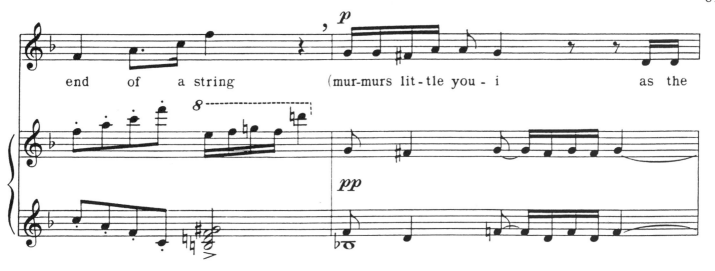

end of a string (mur-murs lit-tle you - i as the

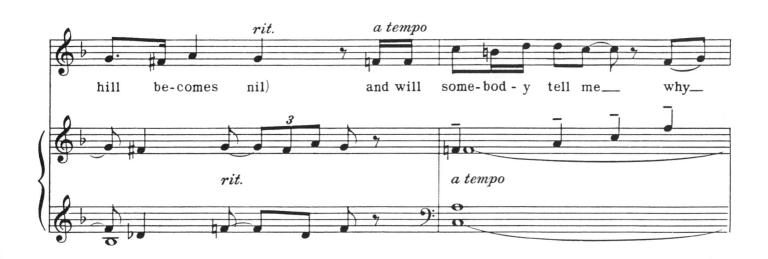

hill be-comes nil) and will some-bod-y tell me__ why__

peo-ple let go

PIANISSIMO

Eli Ives Collins*

Celius Dougherty

*Words printed by special permission.

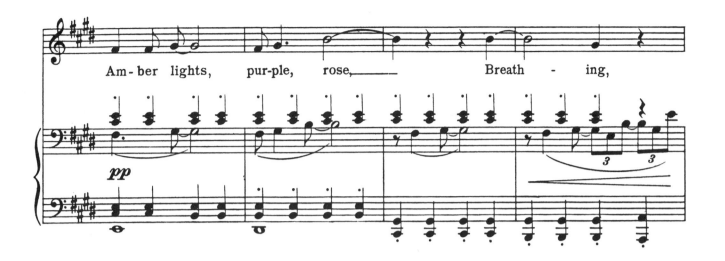

Am - ber lights, pur-ple, rose,_____ Breath - ing,

Breath - ing the mu - sic goes._____

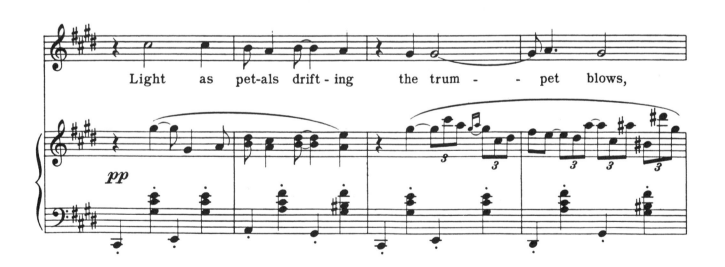

Light as pet-als drift - ing the trum - - pet blows,

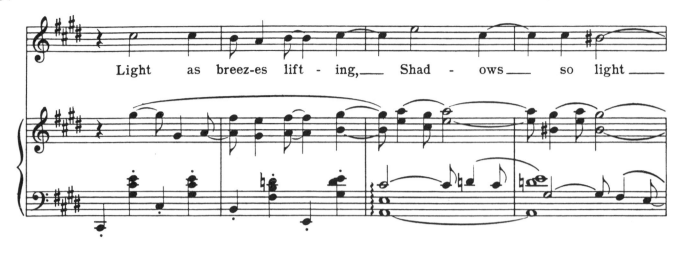

Light as breez-es lift - ing,___ Shad - ows___ so light___

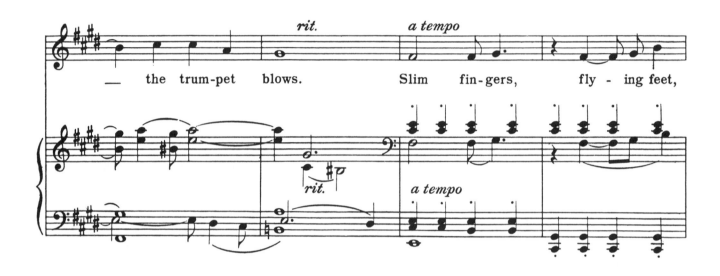

_ the trum-pet blows. Slim fin-gers, fly - ing feet,

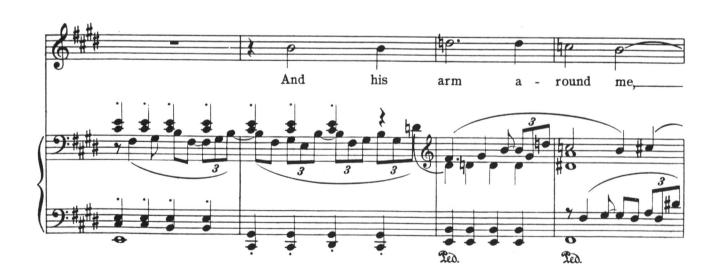

And his arm a - round me,___

And the beat___ and the throb___ of the

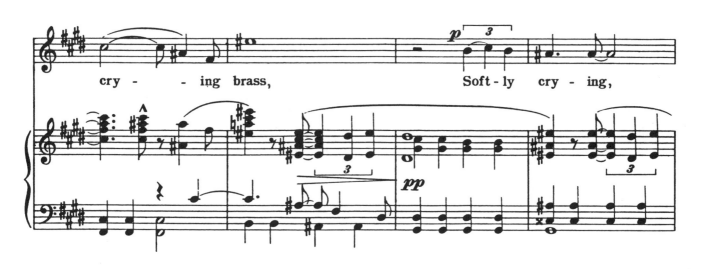

cry - - ing brass, Soft - ly cry - ing,

soft - ly dy - ing; And the beat___ and the

throb of the cry - - ing brass, soft - ly

cry - ing, soft - ly dy - ing. And the

mo-ments pass,___ and it's got to end. So soft___

he_ dan-ces, so strong _____ and_ soft, like the

lan-terns sway-ing up_____ a - loft;

And I like his breath - ing in my hair,____

And the mu-sic stops,____ and I care,_____ I

care,_____ I care._____

PRIMAVERA

Amy Lowell*

Celius Dougherty

* Poem from "What's O'clock," published by Houghton Mifflin Company. Used by permission.

say - ing____ that it is five good days to the twenty-first of

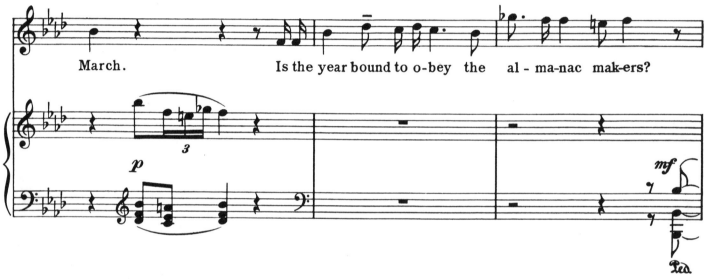

March. Is the year bound to o-bey the al - ma-nac mak-ers?

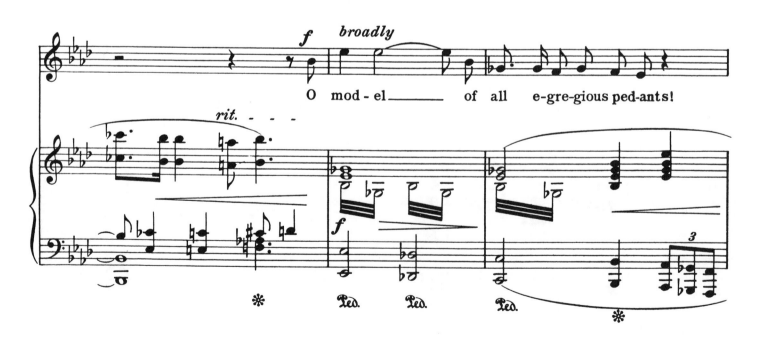

O mod - el____ of all e-gre-gious ped-ants!

Would you shackle Spring   to times   and seasons,

And catch her   back   by her long green skirt Till the

moment you have planned for her?

She has

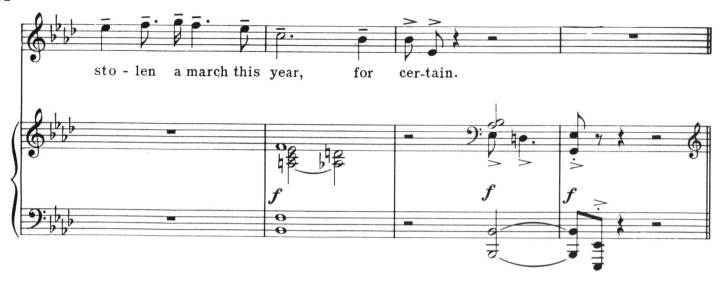

sto - len   a march this year,   for   cer-tain.

Rhythmic ♩ = 128-132

without pedal

short pedals ad libitum

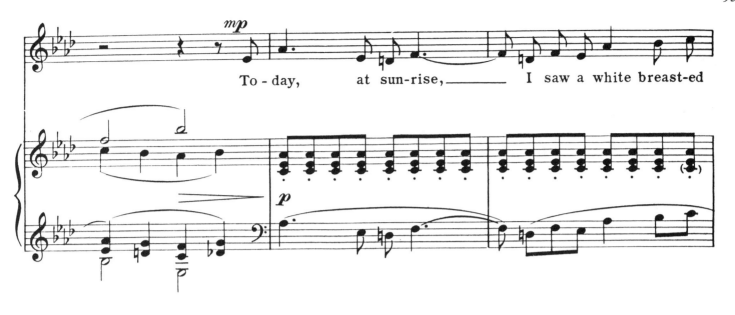

To - day, at sun-rise,_____ I saw a white breast-ed

nut - hatch running up the branch of the oak - tree_____ That was so

bro - ken by the ice-storm last De - cem - ber,

And in the gar - den a pheas - ant____ was picking grains Out of the ma-

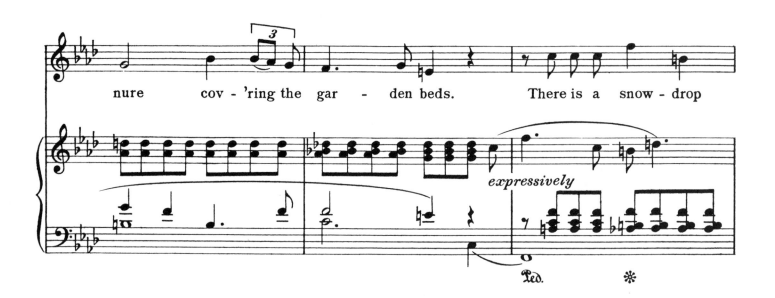

nure cov - 'ring the gar - den beds. There is a snow - drop

expressively

Ped. ✻

up by the porch, Shot clean through the tu - lip straw;

Ped.

And the crows are all a-gog o-ver my neigh-bor's pine trees.

It is a game of catch-who-catch-can with that

green skirt then. E-ven though,

mf

allarg.

f very rhythmic

be-yond the shad - ow of a doubt,

I saw the Spring.

PORTRAIT

Robert Browning

Celius Dougherty

flash a-cross: Vio - lets were born!

Sky, what a scowl of cloud,

Till,____ near____ and far,____ Ray____ on ray

split the shroud: Splen - did,   a star!

World!_____   how it walled   a-

bout   Life_____ with   dis - grace____

REVIEW

Celius Dougherty

Allegro maestoso

Last night in Car-ne-gie Hall _ Miss Sa-da-belle Smith, _ so-

pra - no, gave her first New York re - cit - al _____ be - fore a

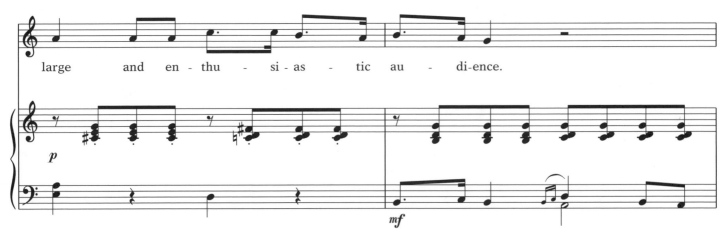

large and en - thu - si - as - tic au - di-ence.

The words of this song were excerpted, adapted and paraphrased from actual reviews.

Blessed with a hand - some stage pres-ence and a
rich and _____ gor - geous voice, the gift - ed
sing - er im-pressed as an art - ist _____ of re - fine - ment and __
rare _____ dis - tinc - tion.

And though the sing-er could be com- mend-ed for a cer - tain grasp of style, the voice sel - dom es - caped a throat - y spread ___ type of pro - duc - tion.

sostenuto

con Ped.

rit.

a tempo

f

And a-gain through fault - y breath sup-port and in - suf-fi - cient use of the di - a-phragm, the tones were un - fo-cused and thin and some-times e - ven na - sal.

But   it   was when   she reached her op - er - at - ic   se - lec-tions

broaden

that Miss   Smith   was   on   fa - mil   -   iar

in tempo

ground.

Now the voice be - came more firm - ly an - chored, more point - ed, and de - cid - ed-ly rich - er in tex-ture, the tones in the low - er part of the com-pass match - ing in qual - i - ty those a - bove.

The sounds pro-duced were no-ta-bly free and for-ward, she poured forth her glam-our-ous tones at the full; They were op-u-lent, vel-vet-y,

and sure in mat-ters of fo-cus and pitch, and _

e - ven _ in _ scale _____ through-

out. She boast - ed

un - u - su - al ___ in - tel - li-gence,

at a song _____ re -

cit - al.

ff

Max Schmidt was the sym - pa - thet - ic ac - com - pa - nist.

p

pp

SERENADER

George Dillon*   Celius Dougherty

*Words from BOY IN THE WIND by George Dillon, Copyright 1927 by The Viking Press, Inc.

It is a song_____ that I have made._____ Now in your keep - ing_____ it is laid._____

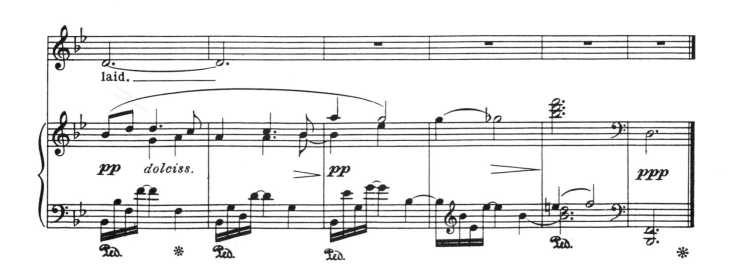

SONATINA

Rose Fyleman*

Celius Dougherty

* **Words from** *Fairies and Chimneys* **by Rose Fyleman, Copyright, 1920, by Doubleday & Company, Inc.**

though I'm sure they're ver - y good; I

don't like por-ridge, though my Na - na says I

should; I don't like the spi - ders in the at-tic where I

play; And the fun-ny noise the

bath makes   When the wa - ter   runs a - way.

I don't like the feel-ing

when my gloves   are made   of   silk,   And I

don't like the sli - my, skin-ny stuff on the top of hot

milk; I don't like ti-gers, not e-ven in a book,

faster

And I

f *broader*

know it's ver-y naugh-ty but I don't like cook.

SONG FOR AUTUMN

Mary Webb

Celius Dougherty

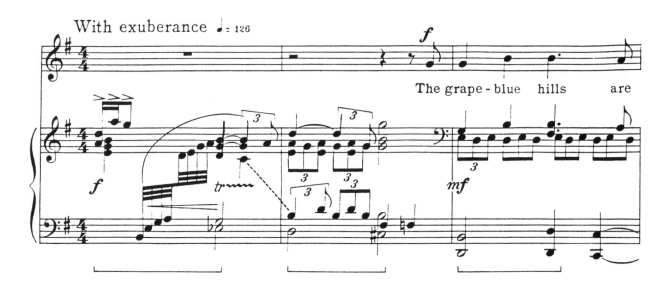

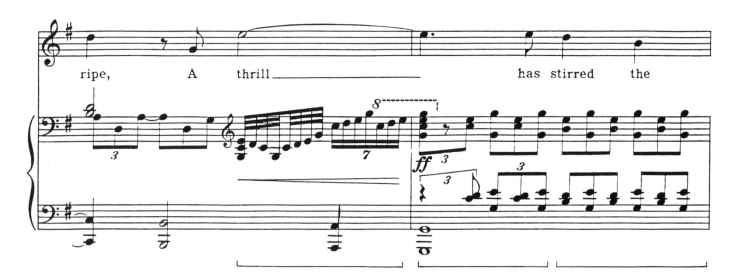

fool - ish, chat-ter - ing__ birds, be still:

My lov - er's gone.
(love is)

Thun - der_____ is on the fields and fear,

No thrush-es sing,_____ And

no bees_____ hum,_____

But

SOUND THE FLUTE!

William Blake

Celius Dougherty

Quickly and lightly ♪ = 184

Sound the Flute! Now it's mute. Birds de-light Day and Night;

Night-in-gale In the dale, Lark in Sky, Out of sight;

Mer-ri-ly, Mer-ri-ly, Mer-ri-ly, To wel-come in the Year.

Lit-tle Boy, Full of Joy; Lit-tle Girl, Sweet and small;

sempre **pp**

Cock does crow, So do you; Mer-ry voice, In-fant noise;

Mer-ri-ly, Mer-ri-ly, Mer-ri-ly, To wel-come in the Year.

THE STRANGER

from the Gaelic

Celius Dougherty

128

TAPESTRY

William Douglas*

Celius Dougherty

*Poem reprinted by permission from *The Atlantic Monthly*

rit. - - - - *a tempo*

young, By some en - chant - ment herd - ed, Be -

rit. - - - - *a tempo*

neath the bam - boo trees, Whose stems with light were

gird - ed In flick -'ring fan - - ta - sies.

mf

espressivo

f

And as I stood there

dim. e rit.

a tempo

gaz - ing, In sun - light and in shade, They

raised small heads from graz - ing, With soft eyes un - a - fraid. I

rit. *a tempo*

rit. *a tempo*

could not pull my gold - en dart____ Out of its broi-der'd

case; It seemed as if my ver - y heart were si - lent

in its place.

thy fingers make early flowers

e.e. cummings

Celius Dougherty

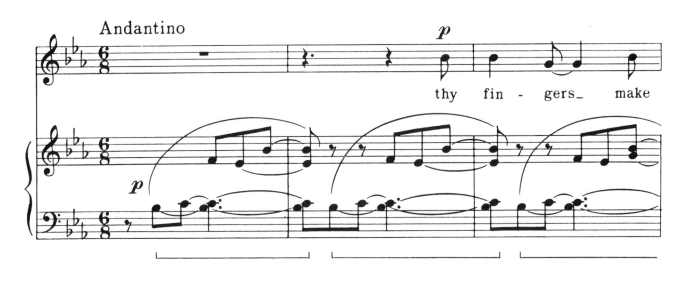

say - ing—   (though love be   a   day)

do not fear,   we will go— a - may - ing.—

thy whit - est   feet   crisp - ly   are stray - ing.

bring - ing?

to

be thy lips is a sweet thing and small.____

a tempo
pp espressivo

Death thee i call rich____ be - yond wish - ing____ if

this thou catch, else miss-ing. (though love be a day

and life be noth-ing,

it___ shall not stop kiss-ing).

until and i heard

e.e. cummings

Celius Dougherty

truth is a cry_____ of_____ a whole_____ of a

soul un-

til i a-woke_____ for the beau-ti-ful sake_____ of a

grave _____ gay _____ brave _____ bright

cry of a - live _____ with a trill _____

like _____ un - til

UPSTREAM

Carl Sandburg*

Celius Dougherty

* **Words used by permission**

strong moth-ers pull-ing them on. _____ The strong moth-ers

pull-ing them from a dark sea, _____ a

great prai - rie, _____ a long moun - tain. _____

Call hal - le-

WEATHERS

Thomas Hardy*

Celius Dougherty

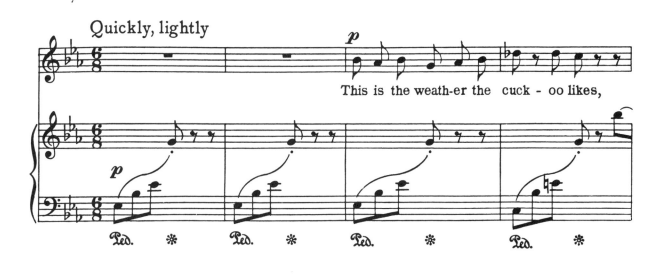

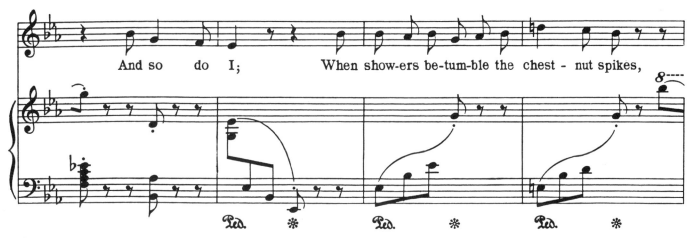

lit-tle brown night-in-gale bills his best, And they

sit out-side at "the Trave-ler's Rest", And

maids step forth_ in mus-lin drest, And

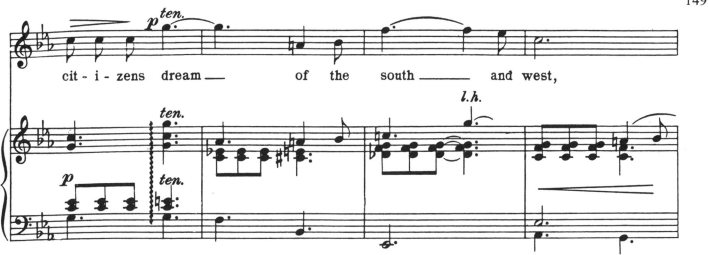

cit - i - zens dream ____ of the south ____ and west,

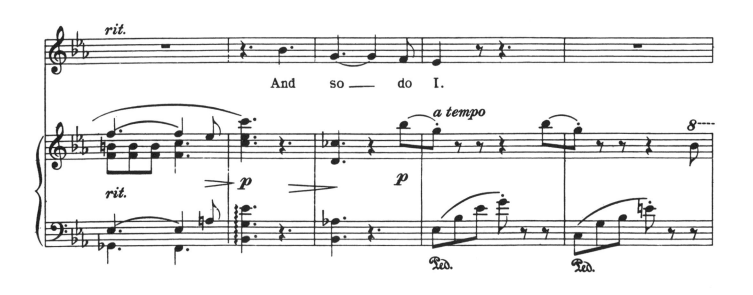

And so ___ do I.

This is the weath-er the shep-herd shuns,

And so — do I; When beech-es drip in browns and duns

And thresh — and ply;

And hill - hid tides throb throe ___ on throe, And

mea - dow riv - u -lets o - ver-flow, And drops ___ on

gate - bars hang in a row, And

rooks _____ in fam - 'lies home - - ward go, _____ And so _____ do

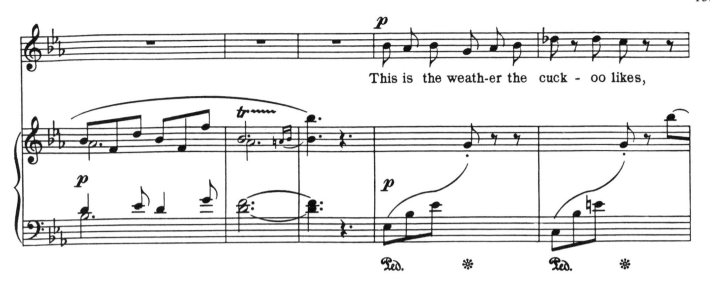

This is the weath-er the cuck - oo likes,

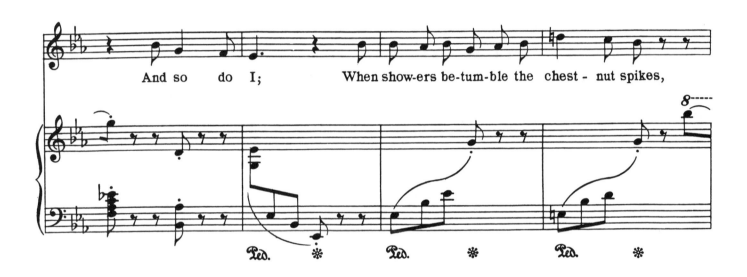

And so do I; When show-ers be-tum-ble the chest - nut spikes,

And nest-lings fly; _____ And the

lit-tle brown night-in-gale bills his best, And they

sit out-side at "The Trave-ler's Rest", And

maids step forth in mus-lin drest, And

cit-i-zens dream ____ of the south ____ and west,

And so ____ do I. _____

WHAT THE BULLET SANG

Bret Harte

Celius Dougherty